# REPORT OF THE NATIONAL COMMISSION FOR THE REVIEW OF THE RESEARCH AND DEVELOPMENT PROGRAMS OF THE UNITED STATES INTELLIGENCE COMMUNITY

## UNCLASSIFIED VERSION

## Glossary

A variety of terms pertaining to scientific and technical research and development are employed by the Intelligence Community (IC) and in this report. Key concepts in this report are:

**Enhanced Integrated Intelligence (EII)** – EII is the rearchitecturing of collection and analysis processes enabled by automated collection, analysis, integration, and discovery of relevant intelligence data and information from classified and open sources. The goal is to achieve a better contextual understanding of the world. EII extends the integration of intelligence capabilities—begun under the Intelligence Reform and Terrorism Prevention Act of 2004 (IRTPA) and continued by the unification of collection and analysis under a single Deputy Director of National Intelligence—to include the research and development activities that support collection and analysis.

**Scientific and Technical Intelligence (also Science and Technology Intelligence or Scientific and Technological Intelligence; abbreviated S&TI)** – S&TI is the systematic study and analysis of foreign capabilities in basic and applied research and applied engineering. S&TI products are used to warn of foreign technical developments and capabilities and to guide the development of future capabilities, which are often provided through R&D. In this report, S&TI is understood more broadly: it includes not only the efforts described above but also aspects of counterintelligence and open-source intelligence used to provide a comprehensive picture of global scientific and technological advancements.

Each of the following terms, though sometimes used interchangeably, has a distinct meaning:

**Research and Technology (R&T or RT)** – RT is an expenditure center within the National Intelligence Program (NIP) budget that funds many of the activities within the IC R&D enterprise.

**Research and Development (R&D)** – As used in the IC, R&D is a broad term encompassing all of the intelligence and intelligence-related work systematically undertaken to develop new scientific and technical knowledge and to apply such knowledge in developing or improving existing applications (sensors, devices, analytical tools, and so on). Acquisition is not typically part of development.

**Research, Development, Test, and Evaluation (RDT&E)** – RDT&E is a Department of Defense (DOD) budget appropriation that covers the entire development cycle, from basic research through final operational test. At the conclusion of RDT&E, the system is ready for procurement and fielding to the operators.

**Science and Technology (S&T)** – S&T is a broad term for the entire range of scientific and technical disciplines used to codify, increase, or apply knowledge. In the IC, S&T generally describes the knowledge that is developed and applied to IC mission needs. In the DOD, S&T refers specifically to basic research, applied research, and the advanced development of knowledge and of system prototypes.

*Failure to properly appraise the extent of scientific developments in enemy countries may have more immediate and catastrophic consequences than failure in any other field of intelligence.*

—Task Force Report on National Security Organization (the Eberstadt Report) (1948)

*Failure to properly <u>resource and use our own R&D to appraise, exploit, and counter</u> the scientific and technical developments of our adversaries—including both state and non-state actors— may have more immediate and catastrophic consequences than failure in any other field of intelligence.*

—National Commission for the Review of the Research and Development Programs of the United States Intelligence Community (2013)

This page intentionally left blank.

# Contents

This page intentionally left blank.

# Preface

**CO-CHAIRS:**

Mr. Maurice Sonnenberg

Samantha Ravich, PhD


**COMMISSIONERS:**

Sen. Dan Coats

Rep. Mike Conaway

Rep. Rush Holt

Hon. Shirley Ann Jackson, PhD

Mr. Gilman Louie

Mr. Kevin Meiners

Hon. Stephanie O'Sullivan

Mr. Troy Wade

Sen. Mark Warner

Hon. John J. Young, Jr.


**EXECUTIVE DIRECTOR:**

David A. Bray, PhD

Since Congress created the modern Intelligence Community (IC) with the passage of the National Security Act of 1947, the IC has existed to serve one overarching goal—to provide timely and accurate intelligence to inform, warn, and act on behalf of U.S. decisionmakers to ensure our continued national security. The National Commission for the Review of the Research and Development Programs of the United States Intelligence Community was established by Public Law 107-306, as amended by Public Law 111-259, to review the R&D programs of the IC and to ensure that this goal is being, and will continue to be, met.

In the legislation establishing the Commission, Congress noted that for the foreseeable future, the IC "must operate in a dynamic, highly-challenging environment against a growing number of hostile, technically-sophisticated threats." Aided by their growing national commitments to R&D, current and potential adversaries of U.S. interests have easy access to advanced sensors, social media tools, a variety of communication networks, precision weapons and home-made devices, analytical software, and many other capabilities for undermining our national advantage. IC R&D programs are critical to ensure that the United States advances and maintains "technological capabilities to detect, characterize, assess, and ultimately counter the full range of threats to the national security of the United States."

The Commission conducted a thorough review of the IC R&D enterprise, including its relationship with the broader U.S. R&D base and the U.S. R&D talent pool. The Commission held individual sessions with R&D leaders and national security experts from the IC, Department of Defense, Executive Office of the President, academia, and private industry and also reviewed policies and programs aimed at enhancing the nation's science, technology, engineering, and mathematics (STEM) workforce. Several IC-wide data calls were conducted to gain information about current IC R&D budgets as well as R&D priorities. The Commission also reviewed five IC R&D topics to consider illustrative areas of high interest in more detail.

1

There are two key challenges that Congress and the IC must address to ensure U.S. national security. First, the global diffusion of R&D efforts is accelerating, posing increasing risk to the essential capabilities of the IC and to national security. Second, the ever-increasing sophistication of our adversaries—coupled with the growing volume and complexity of the data collected—is testing the ability of the IC R&D enterprise to succeed in its mission absent greater Community-wide integration and leadership. To address these challenges, Congress and IC leadership must ensure that R&D is recognized as a critical and strategic component of the IC's missions—and empower the IC R&D enterprise to act accordingly.

We echo previous congressional commissions and prominent studies as we stress that complementing our above concerns is the need for Congress to better protect and prepare the broader U.S. industrial base through legislation focused on improving STEM education, creating skills-based immigration policies, securing the supply chains of critical materials and technologies, and countering cyber theft and foreign espionage.

*Like traditional national security issues, these R&D issues transcend partisanship, and, for the good of our nation, Congress should act to address these concerns.*

# Summary of Findings and Recommendations

The global spread of scientific and technical knowledge challenges U.S. national security. It threatens to erode essential capabilities of the U.S. Intelligence Community (IC) and the strength of the U.S. R&D base.

The IC has played a vital role in maintaining the United States' global preeminence. Over the years, its successes have been underpinned by R&D achievements in the private and public sectors, some of which were directly supported by research programs sponsored by the federal government. From the first mass data storage and retrieval systems to satellites to the mathematics of modern cryptography, public- and private-sector R&D has been crucial to the ability of the IC to perform and succeed in its missions.

But today U.S. technological superiority is diminishing in important areas, and our adversaries' investments in S&T—along with their theft of our intellectual property, made possible in part by insufficient cyber protection and policies—are giving them new, asymmetric advantages. The United States faces increasing risk from threats against which the IC could have severely limited warning, deterrence, or agility to develop effective countermeasures.

## *The Threat from Global Scientific and Technical Knowledge*

Our adversaries' use of S&T increasingly challenges IC capabilities in critical areas, including:

- *Cryptography.* The availability and strength of high-grade encryption schemes continue to expand.
- *Assured Space Access.* Foreign countries continue to develop new technologies and methods for disrupting our space assets, necessitating the development of resilient approaches.
- *Cyber Attack and Defense.* As cyber attacks grow in scale and scope, we struggle to defend against this rising threat.
- *Nuclear Technology and Forensics.* The proliferation of nuclear materials and technology will remain a high-priority national security threat.
- *Global Supply Chains.* Production and distribution chains are increasingly vulnerable to a variety of actions, including intentional disruptions.
- *All-Source Data Analytics.* The volume of data is challenging our ability to process and use it.

Exacerbating these challenges are U.S. policies that weaken the U.S. R&D talent base. As scientific and technical knowledge and the resulting economic growth spread around the world, the competition for R&D talent is increasingly global. Other countries have committed significant resources to pursue R&D in areas such as quantum computing, physics, materials, energy, all-source data analytics, biomedical sciences, and pharmaceuticals. The United States is increasingly losing talent as foreign students and professors who have been educated and employed in the United States return to their home countries or move overseas to pursue their research in places where they find modern equipment and laboratories, less bureaucracy and administrative red tape, and more attractive compensation. These trends are further complicated by the diminished support for R&D by the U.S. government.

Given the scope and accelerating pace of global R&D activities, the IC must change and broaden its strategy for how it pursues innovative ideas. First, for areas in which it is essential that the United States maintain superiority (e.g., cryptography), the IC must maintain its R&D base. Second, when needed innovations may be obtained from the broader U.S. R&D base, the IC must encourage more participants—particularly small, innovative firms. Such firms currently are often discouraged or precluded from contributing by the time and cost imposed by the IC's security and procurement requirements, not to mention the onerous restrictions placed on them as subcontractors of some of the larger contracting organizations.[1] A tiered approach that allows more direct contracting with small firms for important R&D areas should be examined, with the goal of applying it broadly across the IC R&D enterprise. Finally, for areas of basic research—that is, research that is often unclassified—the IC must aggressively leverage the global talent pool.

### *Strategic Objectives and Challenges*

To ensure that the United States prevails in a global environment in which our adversaries have access to advanced scientific and technical knowledge at a level approaching, and sometimes higher than, that possessed by the United States, the Commission finds that the IC must (1) uncover global threats more completely and at an early stage, and (2) be more agile, more aggressive, and faster in how it develops innovative, new capabilities.

The Commission underscores four challenges to achieving the principal objectives of uncovering global threats more completely and being more agile in developing new capabilities: the IC must *broaden scientific and technical intelligence, enhance integrated intelligence, empower R&D leadership,* and *leverage expertise and talent wherever it resides.*

---

[1] "Small Businesses Face an Imperfect Federal Contracting System," Free Enterprise, 28 August 2012, p. 1, www.freeenterprise.com/small-businesses-face-imperfect-federal-contracting-system (accessed 21 Feb. 2013). The time and expense of contracting can even put small concerns out of business; Vicky W. Knerly, "Contracting with the U.S. Government: A Small Business Perspective," www.ago noaa.gov/docs/small_business_contracting_with_the_government.pdf (accessed 21 Feb. 2013).

## Broaden Scientific and Technical Intelligence

*Finding 1:* The Commission found a limited effort by the IC to discern and exploit the strategic R&D—especially non-military R&D—intentions and capabilities of our adversaries, and to counter our adversaries' theft or purchase of U.S. technology.

*Recommendation 1:* Conduct comprehensive strategic scientific and technical intelligence (S&TI); use it for IC R&D planning and resource allocation.

## Enhance Integrated Intelligence

*Finding 2:* The Commission found that while the traditional ways and means of collecting and analyzing intelligence remain useful and necessary, emerging and future threats cannot be addressed without Enhanced Integrated Intelligence capabilities that enable shared, discoverable data for analysis and shared, discoverable information for decisionmakers.

*Recommendation 2:* Focus advanced IC R&D on Enhanced Integrated Intelligence approaches— methods that integrate diverse sources and expertise and that employ automated capabilities to tag, discover, access, and aggregate both data and analyzed information.

## Empower R&D Leadership

*Finding 3:* The Commission found that there is inadequate IC R&D strategic planning and inadequate awareness of IC R&D investment plans and programs.

*Recommendation 3:* Empower IC R&D leadership to develop a comprehensive R&D strategy and oversee R&D resource allocation.

## Leverage People/Talent

*Finding 4:* The Commission found substantial interest within the IC to take advantage of talent and innovation in both the domestic and international private sectors, as well as within the IC itself, but the IC must evolve its business and personnel practices to leverage and exploit the STEM personnel marketplace.

*Recommendation 4:* Assess longer-term workforce needs within the context of a more competitive private sector and global marketplace and develop procedures to recruit and keep needed talent. Increase and augment IC R&D talent by emphasizing approaches to innovation sharing within the public and private sectors, universities, and research and national labs, and by developing an IC strategy and approach for creating R&D opportunities for non-U.S. citizens.

## _Broaden Scientific and Technical Intelligence_

The increasing pace and adoption of global scientific and technological discovery heighten the risk of strategic or tactical surprise and, over time, reduce the advantages of our intelligence capabilities. To counter these effects, the strategy of the IC first must be to seek global knowledge of—as well as influence over and access to—R&D developments. The Commission's first finding is that the IC is not adequately assessing the strategic R&D intentions and capabilities of our adversaries. The recommendation is therefore to expand the effort devoted to scientific and technical intelligence (S&TI), and to use the insights thereby gained to develop new capabilities and understand the strategic intent of these actors' S&T investments.

### Finding 1: Limited Effort to Discern and Exploit Adversaries' Strategic R&D Intentions

_Investment in, and development of, sophisticated technology by other nations and the private sector, as well as access to technology developed by others, is increasing. Scientific breakthroughs outside the United States, often accomplished with U.S. talent or technology, are enabling rapid innovation in a number of strategic sectors.[2] Inadequate IC awareness of and access to global R&D likely will make the nation more vulnerable to the loss of vital and unique national security capabilities, as well as vulnerable to new adversary capabilities._

Rapid growth of global R&D exceeds the IC's ability to understand, access, and develop countering technologies. The limited ability of the IC to know, understand, and evaluate global R&D and its effects on the national and economic security of the United States was a theme often discussed in Commission meetings with leaders, managers, and experts on the IC and R&D. Yet it is difficult to discern significant changes in plans or programs made in response to the globalization of R&D. Such urgency was seen in the aftermath of the 1948 Task Force Report on National Security Organization (the Eberstadt Report), which noted the critical importance of understanding scientific advancements outside the United States.[3]

In the mid-20th century, the United States relied on groundbreaking R&D to confront a grave threat. The development and deployment of the strategic reconnaissance satellites of the

---

[2] For example, Czech scientists at the Technical University of Liberec have discovered a technology for the weaving of nanofibers (http://czech.cz/en/Education/Science-and-research/Czech-scientific-successes/the-most-significant-current-discoveries, accessed 14 Feb. 2013); Chinese researchers in Guangdong Province have confirmed and measured a third type of neutrino oscillation ("Frugality Fuels Science Breakthrough," China.org.cn, 6 February 2013, www.china.org.cn/china/2013-02/context_27906693.htm, accessed 14 Feb. 2013); and physicists at CERN report discovering the Higgs Boson particle (Robert T. Gonzalez, "Physicists Reveal Compelling Evidence for the 'God Particle,'" io9, 13 December 2011, http://io9.com/5867512/two-independent-cern-experiments-are-closing-in-on-the-higgs-boson, accessed 14 Feb. 2013).

[3] See this volume's first epigraph, quoted in Department of State, _Foreign Relations of the United States, 1945–1959: Emergence of the Intelligence Establishment_, ed. C. Thomas Thorne Jr. and David S. Patterson, general ed. Glenn W. LaFantasie (Washington, DC: U.S. Government Printing Office, 1996), p. 1012. Ferdinand Eberstadt headed the Hoover Commission Task Force on National Security Organization, part of the larger Commission on Organization of the Executive Branch of the Government established by President Truman.

CORONA program gave the United States the ability, for the first time, to regularly see into the Soviet Union on a grand scale. CORONA provided the foundation for nearly all space-based mapping technologies developed over the past 50 years—from the street maps available on the personal devices we use in our daily lives to weather maps that enable us to compare changes in global climate.[4] None of this would have been possible without a solid R&D base, strategic focus, and vision. Without continuing dedication to R&D, and to the men and women who work in R&D, the United States will not develop the CORONAs of the future.[5]

Currently, the Director of National Intelligence (DNI) organizes responsibilities for collection and analysis across 15 National Intelligence Managers, each of whom produces a Unifying Intelligence Strategy. The office of the National Intelligence Manager for S&T (NIM-S&T) has the mission of appraising the extent of scientific developments throughout the world—but does not focus sufficiently on global private industry, where many of the advances are being made. The limitations on assessing global S&T are largely due to the rapid increase in the globalization of R&D and to the NIM-S&T's not stressing these types of foreign activities.

Foreign governments are developing policies to foster technological innovation as a key mechanism for stimulating sustainable economic growth and enhancing security—the fruits of which will present both challenges to and opportunities for U.S. interests. The globalization of R&D capabilities is becoming an increasingly important component of the business strategies of multinational corporations, not only because they wish to boost competitiveness by enhancing local customization, gaining access to new markets, and placing technical staff close to manufacturing and design centers, but also because the accelerating pace of S&T-based innovation and its potential for high-margin products drive successful firms to seek out the best S&T talent, regardless of where it resides.

Foreign economic espionage is helping both adversaries and allies.[6] The U.S. government must act to stem the economic and national security risks posed by large-scale espionage, which often is state-sponsored.

Foreign countries' growing expertise and proficiency in a number of emerging or potentially disruptive technologies and industries—gained either by improving their own capabilities, by using surreptitious methods, or by taking advantage of an erosion of U.S. capabilities and U.S. control over critical supply chains—have the potential to cause great harm to the national security of the United States and its allies. Of equal concern, foreign nations can acquire early-stage U.S. technology and start-up companies, through venture capital investment or acquisition—in areas whose future national security and economic implications may not yet

---

[4] Frederic C. E. Oder, James C. Fitzpatrick, and Paul E. Worthman, *The Corona Story* (Washington, DC: National Reconnaissance Office, 1997).

[5] See Robert A. McDonald, *Corona: Success for Space Reconnaissance; A Look into the Cold War and a Revolution for Intelligence* (Washington, DC: National Reconnaissance Office, 1995).

[6] Office of the National Counterintelligence Executive (ONCIX), "Foreign Spies Stealing US Economic Secrets in Cyberspace: Report to Congress on Foreign Economic Collection and Industrial Espionage, 2009–2011," October 2011, p. 7; *2012 Report to Congress of the U.S.-China Economic and Security Review Commission* (Washington, DC: U.S. Government Printing Office, 2012), p. 148.

be appropriately and fully recognized. Current U.S. policies on, and mechanisms to review, foreign ownership and control of U.S. companies or U.S.-affiliated companies (most prominently, the Committee on Foreign Investment in the United States, or CFIUS) have not kept pace with the evolution of business practices in the high-technology market.

## Recommendation 1: Conduct comprehensive strategic scientific and technical intelligence (S&TI); use it for IC R&D planning and resource allocation

*Improve the IC's comprehension of foreign strategies for science and technology developments through scientific and technical intelligence, and use this knowledge to help construct IC requirements, programs, and threat assessments. Ensure that S&TI requirements inform the development and integration of multidisciplinary tools and functions throughout the IC R&D enterprise, including allocations of IC R&D resources.*

### Actions for Recommendation 1

1.1 IC R&D budget requests to Congress must include annual S&TI assessments for major areas of investment.

1.2 The Office of the Director of National Intelligence must identify IC S&TI priorities. ODNI will incorporate this input when creating applicable Unifying Intelligence Strategy (UIS) documents.

1.3 When relevant, IC assessments provided to Congress should include S&TI assessments—including assessments of counterintelligence (CI) against IC R&D—along with comparisons to IC R&D priorities. These serve as justification for future IC R&D requirements and activities, and help inform IC engagement with the industrial base.

### First-Year Accomplishments

After one year the Commission expects the IC to have at least:

- Created an appropriately sized S&TI cell—increasing the emphasis on open-source information in the assessment of foreign S&T, and augmenting, training, and recruiting expertise in science, engineering, and business
- Established S&TI requirements based on intelligence gaps and incorporated these requirements into the applicable Unifying Intelligence Strategies
- Developed and implemented the process for ensuring that S&TI is utilized by the IC R&D enterprise

## *Enhance Integrated Intelligence*

The speed with which an adversary can acquire and exploit scientific and technical knowledge continues to increase. In addition to posing new threats that are fast-forming or that have low signatures, adversaries have learned to conceal their operations from the IC and have developed an awareness of U.S. capabilities. It is imperative that the Intelligence Community develop ways to gain and exploit insights earlier and faster.

The key finding is that the current method of producing IC intelligence—collecting information and integrating it afterward—loses valuable time and information. The collection and analysis process is becoming at once more difficult, given the increase in the scale and diversity of information sources, and more essential, given the intelligence significance of the explosive growth in access to and operations in cyberspace. The recommendation focuses on how to realize Enhanced Integrated Intelligence—comprising the automated collection, analysis, integration, and discovery of relevant data and information—in which decision cycles can occur in near real time.

### Finding 2: Enhanced Integrated Intelligence Needed for Emerging and Future Threats

*The global environment in which the IC must operate and dominate is changing. Fast-forming and low-signal threats, including "do-it-yourself" capabilities and economic espionage, are becoming the norm along with rising state challengers and super-empowered non-state actors. The IC must make the coordinated tasking, aggregation, and integrated processing and sharing of data from multiple sources a priority to provide collated signals of adversary actions and intentions that would be missed if the single-source threads of intelligence were reviewed individually.*

To meet the challenge of scalable Enhanced Integrated Intelligence, the IC must, for example, develop or expand capabilities for agile, synchronized tasking, collection, and analysis across intelligence disciplines (signals intelligence [SIGINT], human intelligence [HUMINT], etc.) and across collection domains (space, air, ground, subsurface). Approaches to analysis must be developed that use all available information, thereby enabling the IC to better anticipate developments or detect troubling trends at the earliest feasible time. Doing more integrated analysis will require new techniques for data aggregation, tagging, discovery, access, and organization; greater use of "cognitive computing"; high-performance computation; and the leveraging of open-source analysis and multidisciplinary approaches.

There are several barriers to achieving Enhanced Integrated Intelligence. New sources of intelligence-rich data are proliferating worldwide, often driven by commercial and consumer trends. IC practices traditionally have kept the various INTs separate—thereby allowing various IC agencies to develop expertise in specific INTs at the expense of developing strong cross-INT integration. The lack of a strategic R&D approach within the IC limits the investment in long-term research that produces such innovations in intelligence processes.

### Recommendation 2: Enhance Integrated Intelligence

*Focus advanced IC R&D on Enhanced Integrated Intelligence approaches— methods that integrate diverse sources and expertise and that employ automated capabilities to tag, discover, access, and aggregate both data and analyzed information.*

**Actions for Recommendation 2**

2.1 The Office of the Director of National Intelligence must create a new joint program plan between the Director of Science and Technology (DS&T) and the Deputy Director of National Intelligence for Intelligence Integration (DDII) for Enhanced Integrated Intelligence, which it will use to track, prioritize, and coordinate Enhanced Integrated Intelligence R&D across the IC. These priorities will guide multidisciplinary and multi-intelligence R&D efforts.

2.2 ODNI must emphasize R&D for analytical methods to produce warnings that follow from advances in data aggregation, data analytics, the processing of large volumes of data, and predictive analytics.

2.3 ODNI must broaden IC R&D's existing focus so that it also pursues R&D for Enhanced Integrated Intelligence. The Commission recommends an initial pilot program to experiment with emerging capabilities.

**First-Year Accomplishments**

After one year the Commission expects the IC to have at least:

- Generated a comprehensive list of intelligence problems and key investment areas for Enhanced Integrated Intelligence R&D initiatives of the IC; initial priority projects are to define data tagging standards, and to create and implement rules for multilevel data discovery and access

- Established a plan for devoting a baseline percentage of agencies' R&D budgets to pursue Enhanced Integrated Intelligence programs (after a one-year pilot period, ODNI and the heads of the respective agencies should revisit this number on an agency-by-agency basis)

- Created the framework for a dynamic directory of R&D activities and subject matter experts within the IC to better achieve Enhanced Integrated Intelligence objectives

## *Empower R&D Leadership*

The Intelligence Community needs to become more agile, more aggressive, and faster in collecting, analyzing, and developing new offensive and defensive capabilities. Strong R&D leadership is needed to help create new R&D business practices, coordination, planning, and oversight.

The findings detail several factors that hinder the efforts of the R&D enterprise to create a unified plan, among them a set of disparate budgeting schemes and priorities across those IC agencies performing R&D. The ODNI DS&T needs to serve as the lead executive of IC R&D

and provide strategic guidance and coordination to the IC R&D enterprise while valuing the individual agencies' abilities to develop and pursue their own innovative solutions.

## Finding 3: Lack of Unified R&D Emphasis

*The IC has spent a decade supporting immediate military necessities that demand near-term R&D and incremental improvements for specific ends, rather than undertaking strategic endeavors. Strategic R&D goals for the IC enterprise are not jointly established or adopted.[7] With few exceptions, the IC R&D does not adapt rapidly to a changing technology environment.*

IC agencies had difficulty providing the Commission with a financial accounting of their existing and planned R&D projects and budgets. This is a problem rooted in how the IC tracks expenditures (e.g., the practice of incorporating some R&D funding into mission-related efforts).

The Commission recognizes that IC research activities should be classified in a way that appropriately limits the disclosure of sensitive information while ensuring the sharing of innovations. However, the DS&T must have a comprehensive view of the IC R&D enterprise in its entirety.

The Commission identified several challenges that should be addressed. The roles and authorities of the Director of National Intelligence Science and Technology Committee (NISTC) and the ODNI DS&T are not clearly defined in the legislation that created them.[8] The process of coordinating and setting priorities for IC R&D activities has developed slowly. Several IC agencies have their respective areas of expertise and authorities for different types of intelligence, though the coordination of R&D between these agencies can be improved.

## Recommendation 3: Empower R&D Leadership

*Empower IC R&D leadership to develop a comprehensive R&D strategy and oversee R&D resource allocation.*

## Actions for Recommendation 3

3.1 Consolidate the positions of Assistant Deputy Director of National Intelligence for S&T (ADDNI/S&T) and DS&T into the DS&T only. Annually, the DS&T will brief the members of the relevant congressional oversight committees on all relevant issues of R&D, S&T, and R&D acquisition programs. The DNI should establish a budget at a level set by Congress under the

---

[7] Intelligence Science Board, "2010 Science and Technology Task Force: Observations, Findings, and Recommendations," working paper, October 2010, pp. 4–6.

[8] *Intelligence Reform and Terrorism Prevention Act of 2004*, Public Law 108-458, 50 *U.S.C.* §403-3e. The committee's formal name is "Director of National Intelligence Science and Technology Committee," abbreviated as NISTC. The chair of the NISTC is the ODNI DS&T, and its members include the principal science advisors of the National Intelligence Program.

control of the DS&T to facilitate investment in emerging, disruptive, and joint technology projects and in Enhanced Integrated Intelligence.

3.2 Empower the DNI with the authority to annually reprogram R&D project funds, up to a level agreed to by Congress, into existing or new R&D projects without prior notification to Congress for approval.

3.3 Establish a science and technology advisory group for the House Permanent Select Committee on Intelligence (HPSCI)—and reaffirm the value of the Senate Select Committee on Intelligence (SSCI) Technical Advisory Group—to provide independent advice on strategic R&D initiatives, including those that require multiyear funding.

## First-Year Accomplishments

After one year the Commission expects the IC to have at least:

- Developed an improved IC-wide method of tracking research and development efforts and implemented it in time for the FY16 budget build
- Created a unified plan for the IC R&D program that incorporates relevant S&TI and includes a demonstrated means of better aligning IC R&D investments, industry's independent R&D (IRAD), corporate R&D (CRAD), and R&D in academic institutions with U.S. national security objectives
- Established performance metrics for evaluating R&D investments
- Obtained congressional approval for below-threshold reprogramming authority to enable agile R&D investment by the IC

## *Leverage People/Talent*

The continued success of the Intelligence Community depends on a strong, talented scientific and technical workforce. The IC needs innovative approaches to ensure its access to their expertise in the categories and quantities required.

The IC needs to improve how it manages talent so that it keeps workforce skills current, brings in new thinking, and gains the perspectives of experts outside the IC. The IC's R&D workforce historically has concentrated its specialized talent within tightly closed circles. It must change its approach, taking advantage of the opportunities afforded by the expanding global environment to become more adaptable and flexible. The United States must not risk losing our technological lead in a growing number of R&D domains that are critical to our national security.

### Finding 4: Limited Leveraging of the STEM Personnel Marketplace

*Facing increasing competition, the IC can do more to access a larger pool of talent and to leverage the best expertise available in our industries, start-ups,*

*universities, national labs, and federally funded research and development*
*centers (FFRDCs) as well as the S&T/R&D workforce of our allies.*

The IC must better compete for scientific talent in an environment increasingly dominated by globalization. It is expected that this trend in competition will continue, although on a national level the U.S. workforce remains the world's R&D powerhouse. It accounted for about 31 percent of the estimated $1.4 trillion expended on R&D globally in 2012.[9]

The United States' growing reliance on foreign R&D talent must be balanced by increasing the domestic R&D talent base, strengthening STEM education at all levels, and attracting more American STEM undergraduates and graduate students.[10]

Despite its need to draw on outside researchers and research, the IC's ability to leverage, attract, and retain the world's brightest R&D talent continues to be limited by a number of challenges—especially contracting requirements, the need to possess U.S. citizenship to obtain security clearances, the difficulties in obtaining appropriate U.S. visas, and opportunities abroad for U.S. talent.

### Recommendation 4: Increase and Augment IC R&D Talent

*Assess longer-term workforce needs within the context of a more competitive private sector and global marketplace and develop procedures to recruit and keep needed talent. Increase and augment IC R&D talent by emphasizing approaches to innovation sharing within the public and private sectors, universities, and research and national labs, and by developing an IC strategy and approach for creating R&D opportunities for non-U.S. citizens.*

### Actions for Recommendation 4

4.1 Increase the number of industry rotations for talented IC R&D government personnel, covering a broad range of types and sizes of businesses and a range of capabilities of particular interest to the IC. These partnerships should focus on broadening the experiences and deepening the knowledge and insights of both mid- and senior-level government personnel. Improve interaction with small firms by lowering the barriers to entry and by expanding competitions and opportunities for nontraditional providers and innovators to participate in programs.

---

[9]    Battelle, "2012 Global R&D Funding Forecast," December 2011, p. 3; http://battelle.org/docs/default-document-library/2012_global_forecast.pdf (accessed 29 Jan. 2013).

[10]    Anthony P. Carnevale, Nicole Smith, and Michelle Melton, *STEM: Science Technology Engineering and Mathematics* (Washington, DC: Georgetown University, Center on Education and the Workforce, 2012), pp. 6–7; see also National Academy of Sciences, *Rising Above the Gathering Storm: Energizing and Employing America for a Brighter Future* (Washington, DC: National Academies Press, 2012), and National Academy of Sciences, *Assuring the U.S. Department of Defense a Strong Science, Technology, Engineering, and Mathematics (STEM) Workforce* (Washington, DC: National Academies Press, 2012).

4.2 Establish an IC R&D Corps composed primarily of part-time researchers, technologists, scientists, engineers, and entrepreneurs—from the private sector and academia—as well as IC retirees.

4.3 The DNI must identify categories of interest to the IC to aid scientists, researchers, engineers, technologists, S&T analysts, and entrepreneurs seeking fast-track U.S. visas. For select individuals, if clearance procedures allow, such visas should be granted immediately. Create such a fast-track system for both private and government workers. The U.S. government must then determine a process for issuing fast-track visas for S&T and R&D personnel of interest, as is currently done to satisfy business and other needs.

## First-Year Accomplishments

After one year the Commission expects the IC to have at least:

- Created a Strategic Workforce Net Assessment to document the critical scientific and technical skill sets for the IC, and created within the IC human capital system a method of tracking these skill sets

- Increase the flexibility of term-limited appointments to bring in talented outside experts who will transfer skills and know-how to the IC R&D workforce

- Established connections with the Office of Science and Technology Policy (OSTP), the Department of Homeland Security, the Department of State, and the Department of Energy, which will work together in identifying special visa needs of critical importance to the IC while ensuring that counterintelligence and security considerations and investigative procedures remain central to the review process

## *Importance of R&D—Building the Future*

*In the past, the United States has thrived when both our nation and our national security policy have adapted to shape change instead of being shaped by it.*

—2010 National Security Strategy

In the face of the challenges and opportunities presented by globalization, Congress and IC leadership must ensure that R&D is recognized as a critical and strategic component of the IC's missions—and must empower the IC R&D enterprise to act accordingly.

In its review of IC R&D activities, the Commission found that the IC should engage with numerous problems and areas to ensure superiority in the future. The following list illustrates the breadth of R&D that must be undertaken to ensure that the IC's capabilities remain preeminent:

- Quantum information processing
- Advances in high-performance computing
- Real-time sensor data fusion
- Anticipatory analytics from Big Data
- Assured continued nuclear design analysis competency
- Advanced manufacturing
- Creation, maintenance, and detection of cover
- Persistent, agile, and resilient overhead capability
- Artificial intelligence for autonomous system and robotics
- Assured trusted communications
- Detecting and countering foreign media influence
- Understanding human dynamics and complex adaptive systems

This Commission report makes four broad recommendations that must be implemented immediately to protect our future national security by transforming how the IC creates strategic advantage and mitigates the impact of unforeseeable global events.

Just as the 80th U.S. Congress and the Truman administration showed great foresight in passing the National Security Act of 1947, so too the 113th U.S. Congress should promptly make needed reforms to the IC's R&D enterprise and its broader S&TI efforts. It is therefore advised that Congress hold hearings no later than one year after the conclusion of the Commission to ensure that these recommendations are being aggressively pursued and implemented.

This page intentionally left blank.

# Appendices

This page intentionally left blank.

# Abbreviations

| | |
|---|---|
| DNI | Director of National Intelligence |
| DOD | Department of Defense |
| DS&T | Director of Science and Technology |
| EII | Enhanced Integrated Intelligence |
| HUMINT | human intelligence |
| IC | Intelligence Community |
| INT | intelligence |
| JIEDDO | Joint Improvised Explosive Device Defeat Organization |
| NIM-S&T | National Intelligence Manager for Science and Technology |
| ODNI | Office of the Director of National Intelligence |
| R&D | research and development |
| R&T | research and technology |
| RDT&E | research, development, test, and evaluation |
| S&E | science and engineering |
| S&T | science and technology |
| S&TI | scientific and technical intelligence |
| STEM | science, technology, engineering, and mathematics |

# Legislation Pertinent to the Commission

**1. Legislation establishing the Commission from Title 50 of the United States Code**

**NATIONAL COMMISSION FOR REVIEW OF RESEARCH AND DEVELOPMENT PROGRAMS OF THE UNITED STATES INTELLIGENCE COMMUNITY**
Pub. L. 111-259, title VII, § 701(a)(3), Oct. 7, 2010, 124 Stat. 2745, provided that: "The membership of the National Commission for the Review of the Research and Development Programs of the United States Intelligence Community established under subsection (a) of section 1002 of such Act (Public Law 107-306; 50 U.S.C. 401 note) [set out below] (referred to in this section [enacting and amending provisions set out below] as the 'Commission') shall be considered vacant and new members shall be appointed in accordance with such section 1002, as amended by this section." Pub. L. 107-306, title X, Nov. 27, 2002, 116 Stat. 2437, as amended by Pub. L. 108-177, title III, § 315(a), Dec. 13, 2003, 117 Stat. 2610; Pub. L. 111-259, title VII, § 701(a)(1), (4), (b)(3), (c), Oct. 7, 2010, 124 Stat. 2744, 2745, provided that:

### SEC. 1001. FINDINGS.
Congress makes the following findings:
(1) Research and development efforts under the purview of the intelligence community are vitally important to the national security of the United States.
(2) The intelligence community must operate in a dynamic, highly-challenging environment, characterized by rapid technological growth, against a growing number of hostile, technically-sophisticated threats. Research and development programs under the purview of the intelligence community are critical to ensuring that intelligence agencies, and their personnel, are provided with important technological capabilities to detect, characterize, assess, and ultimately counter the full range of threats to the national security of the United States.
(3) There is a need to review the full range of current research and development programs under the purview of the intelligence community, evaluate such programs against the scientific and technological fields judged to be of most importance, and articulate program and resource priorities for future research and development activities to ensure a unified and coherent research and development program across the entire intelligence community.

### SEC. 1002. NATIONAL COMMISSION FOR THE REVIEW OF THE RESEARCH AND DEVELOPMENT PROGRAMS OF THE UNITED STATES INTELLIGENCE COMMUNITY.
**(a) ESTABLISHMENT**.—There is established a commission to be known as the "National Commission for the Review of the Research and Development Programs of the United States Intelligence Community" (in this title referred to as the "Commission").
**(b) COMPOSITION**.—
The Commission shall be composed of 12 members, as follows:
(1) The Principal Deputy Director of National Intelligence.
(2) A senior intelligence official of the Office of the Secretary of Defense, as designated by the Secretary of Defense.

(3) Three members appointed by the majority leader of the Senate, in consultation with the Chairman of the Select Committee on Intelligence of the Senate, one from Members of the Senate and two from private life.

(4) Two members appointed by the minority leader of the Senate, in consultation with the Vice Chairman of the Select Committee on Intelligence of the Senate, one from Members of the Senate and one from private life.

(5) Three members appointed by the Speaker of the House of Representatives, in consultation with the Chairman of the Permanent Select Committee on Intelligence of the House of Representatives, one from Members of the House of Representatives and two from private life.

(6) Two members appointed by the minority leader of the House of Representatives, in consultation with the ranking member of the Permanent Select Committee on Intelligence of the House of Representatives, one from Members of the House of Representatives and one from private life.

**(c) MEMBERSHIP.—**

(1) The individuals appointed from private life as members of the Commission shall be individuals who are nationally recognized for expertise, knowledge, or experience in—

 (A) research and development programs;

 (B) technology discovery and insertion;

 (C) use of intelligence information by national policymakers and military leaders; or

 (D) the implementation, funding, or oversight of the national security policies of the United States.

(2) An official who appoints members of the Commission may not appoint an individual as a member of the Commission if, in the judgment of the official, such individual possesses any personal or financial interest in the discharge of any of the duties of the Commission.

(3) All members of the Commission appointed from private life shall possess an appropriate security clearance in accordance with applicable laws and regulations concerning the handling of classified information.

**(d) CO-CHAIRS.—**

(1) The Commission shall have two co-chairs, selected from among the members of the Commission.

(2) One co-chair of the Commission shall be a member of the Democratic Party, and one co-chair shall be a member of the Republican Party.

(3) The individuals who serve as the co-chairs of the Commission shall be jointly agreed upon by the President, the majority leader of the Senate, the minority leader of the Senate, the Speaker of the House of Representatives, and the minority leader of the House of Representatives.

**(e) APPOINTMENT; INITIAL MEETING.—**

(1) Members of the Commission shall be appointed not later than 45 days after the date of the enactment of this Act [Nov. 27, 2002].

(2) The Commission shall hold its initial meeting on the date that is 60 days after the date of the enactment of this Act.

**(f) MEETINGS; QUORUM; VACANCIES.—**

(1) After its initial meeting, the Commission shall meet upon the call of the co-chairs of the Commission.

(2) Six members of the Commission shall constitute a quorum for purposes of conducting business, except that two members of the Commission shall constitute a quorum for purposes of receiving testimony.

(3) Any vacancy in the Commission shall not affect its powers, but shall be filled in the same manner in which the original appointment was made.

(4) If vacancies in the Commission occur on any day after 45 days after the date of the enactment of this Act [Nov. 27, 2002], a quorum shall consist of a majority of the members of the Commission as of such day.

**(g) ACTIONS OF COMMISSION.—**

(1) The Commission shall act by resolution agreed to by a majority of the members of the Commission voting and present.

(2) The Commission may establish panels composed of less than the full membership of the Commission for purposes of carrying out the duties of the Commission under this title. The actions of any such panel shall be subject to the review and control of the Commission. Any findings and determinations made by such a panel shall not be considered the findings and determinations of the Commission unless approved by the Commission.

(3) Any member, agent, or staff of the Commission may, if authorized by the co-chairs of the Commission, take any action which the Commission is authorized to take pursuant to this title.

**(h) DUTIES.—**

The duties of the Commission shall be—

(1) to conduct, until not later than the date on which the Commission submits the report under section 1007(a), the review described in subsection (i); and

(2) to submit to the congressional intelligence committees, the Director of National Intelligence, and the Secretary of Defense a final report on the results of the review.

**(i) REVIEW.—**

The Commission shall review the status of research and development programs and activities within the intelligence community, including advanced research and development programs and activities.

Such review shall include—

(1) an assessment of the advisability of modifying the scope of research and development for purposes of such programs and activities;

(2) a review of the particular individual research and development activities under such programs;

(3) an evaluation of the current allocation of resources for research and development, including whether the allocation of such resources for that purpose should be modified;

(4) an identification of the scientific and technological fields judged to be of most importance to the intelligence community;

(5) an evaluation of the relationship between the research and development programs and activities of the intelligence community and the research and development programs and activities of other departments and agencies of the Federal Government; and

(6) an evaluation of the relationship between the research and development programs and activities of the intelligence community and the research and development programs and activities of the private sector.

## SEC. 1003. POWERS OF COMMISSION.

**(a) IN GENERAL.—**

(1) The Commission or, on the authorization of the Commission, any subcommittee or member thereof, may, for the purpose of carrying out the provisions of this title—

(A) hold such hearings and sit and act at such times and places, take such testimony, receive such evidence, and administer such oaths; and

(B) require, by subpoena or otherwise, the attendance and testimony of such witnesses and the production of such books, records, correspondence, memoranda, papers, and documents, as the Commission or such designated subcommittee or designated member considers necessary.

(2) Subpoenas may be issued under subparagraph (1)(B) under the signature of the co-chairs of the Commission, and may be served by any person designated by such co-chairs.

(3) The provisions of sections 102 through 104 of the Revised Statutes of the United States (2 U.S.C. 192–194) shall apply in the case of any failure of a witness to comply with any subpoena or to testify when summoned under authority of this section.

**(b) CONTRACTING.—**

The Commission may, to such extent and in such amounts as are provided in advance in appropriation Acts, enter into contracts to enable the Commission to discharge its duties under this title.

**(c) INFORMATION FROM FEDERAL AGENCIES.—**

The Commission may secure directly from any executive department, agency, bureau, board, commission, office, independent establishment, or instrumentality of the Government information, suggestions, estimates, and statistics for the purposes of this title. Each such department, agency, bureau, board, commission, office, establishment, or instrumentality shall, to the extent authorized by law, furnish such information, suggestions, estimates, and statistics directly to the Commission, upon request of the co-chairs of the Commission. The Commission shall handle and protect all classified information provided to it under this section in accordance with applicable statutes and regulations.

**(d) ASSISTANCE FROM FEDERAL AGENCIES.—**

(1) The Director of National Intelligence shall provide to the Commission, on a nonreimbursable basis, such administrative services, funds, staff, facilities, and other support services as are necessary for the performance of the Commission's duties under this title.

(2) The Secretary of Defense may provide the Commission, on a nonreimbursable basis, with such administrative services, staff, and other support services as the Commission may request.

(3) In addition to the assistance set forth in paragraphs (1) and (2), other departments and agencies of the United States may provide the Commission such services, funds, facilities, staff, and other support as such departments and agencies consider advisable and as may be authorized by law.

(4) The Commission shall receive the full and timely cooperation of any official, department, or agency of the United States Government whose assistance is necessary for the fulfillment of the duties of the Commission under this title, including the provision of full and current briefings and analyses.

**(e) PROHIBITION ON WITHHOLDING INFORMATION.—**

No department or agency of the Government may withhold information from the Commission on the grounds that providing the information to the Commission would constitute the unauthorized disclosure of classified information or information relating to intelligence sources or methods.

**(f) POSTAL SERVICES.—**

The Commission may use the United States mails in the same manner and under the same conditions as the departments and agencies of the United States.

**(g) GIFTS.—**

The Commission may accept, use, and dispose of gifts or donations of services or property in carrying out its duties under this title.

## SEC. 1004. STAFF OF COMMISSION.
**(a) IN GENERAL.—**

(1) The co-chairs of the Commission, in accordance with rules agreed upon by the Commission, shall appoint and fix the compensation of a staff director and such other personnel as may be necessary to enable the Commission to carry out its duties, without regard to the provisions of title 5, United States Code, governing appointments in the competitive service, and without regard to the provisions of chapter 51 and subchapter III of chapter 53 of such title relating to classification and General Schedule pay rates, except that no rate of pay fixed under this subsection may exceed the equivalent of that payable to a person occupying a position at level V of the Executive Schedule under section 5316 of such title.

(2) Any Federal Government employee may be detailed to the Commission without reimbursement from the Commission, and such detailee shall retain the rights, status, and privileges of his or her regular employment without interruption.

(3) All staff of the Commission shall possess a security clearance in accordance with applicable laws and regulations concerning the handling of classified information.

**(b) CONSULTANT SERVICES.—**

(1) The Commission may procure the services of experts and consultants in accordance with section 3109 of title 5, United States Code, but at rates not to exceed the daily rate paid a person occupying a position at level IV of the Executive Schedule under section 5315 of such title.

(2) All experts and consultants employed by the Commission shall possess a security clearance in accordance with applicable laws and regulations concerning the handling of classified information.

## SEC. 1005. COMPENSATION AND TRAVEL EXPENSES.
**(a) COMPENSATION.—**

(1) Except as provided in paragraph (2), each member of the Commission may be compensated at not to exceed the daily equivalent of the annual rate of basic pay in effect for a position at level IV of the Executive Schedule under section 5315 of title 5, United States Code, for each day during which that member is engaged in the actual performance of the duties of the Commission under this title.

(2) Members of the Commission who are officers or employees of the United States or Members of Congress shall receive no additional pay by reason of their service on the Commission.

**(b) TRAVEL EXPENSES.—**

While away from their homes or regular places of business in the performance of services for the Commission, members of the Commission may be allowed travel expenses, including per diem in lieu of subsistence, in the same manner as persons employed intermittently in the Government service are allowed expenses under section 5703 of title 5, United States Code.

## SEC. 1006. TREATMENT OF INFORMATION RELATING TO NATIONAL SECURITY.
**(a) IN GENERAL.—**

(1) The Director of National Intelligence shall assume responsibility for the handling and disposition of any information related to the national security of the United States that is received, considered, or used by the Commission under this title.

(2) Any information related to the national security of the United States that is provided to the Commission by a congressional intelligence committee may not be further provided or released without the approval of the chairman of such committee.

**(b) ACCESS AFTER TERMINATION OF COMMISSION.—**

Notwithstanding any other provision of law, after the termination of the Commission under section 1007, only the Members and designated staff of the congressional intelligence committees, the Director of National Intelligence (and the designees of the Director), and such other officials of the executive branch as the President may designate shall have access to information related to the national security of the United States that is received, considered, or used by the Commission.

## SEC. 1007. FINAL REPORT; TERMINATION.

**(a) FINAL REPORT.—**

Not later than one year after the date on which all members of the Commission are appointed pursuant to section 701(a)(3) of the Intelligence Authorization Act for Fiscal Year 2010 [Pub. L. 111-259, set out above], the Commission shall submit to the congressional intelligence committees, the Director of National Intelligence, and the Secretary of Defense a final report as required by section 1002(h)(2).

**(b) TERMINATION.—**

(1) The Commission, and all the authorities of this title, shall terminate at the end of the 120-day period beginning on the date on which the final report under subsection (a) is transmitted to the congressional intelligence committees.

(2) The Commission may use the 120-day period referred to in paragraph (1) for the purposes of concluding its activities, including providing testimony to Congress concerning the final report referred to in that paragraph and disseminating the report.

## SEC. 1008. ASSESSMENTS OF FINAL REPORT.

Not later than 60 days after receipt of the final report under section 1007(a), the Director of National Intelligence and the Secretary of Defense shall each submit to the congressional intelligence committees an assessment by the Director or the Secretary, as the case may be, of the final report. Each assessment shall include such comments on the findings and recommendations contained in the final report as the Director or Secretary, as the case may be, considers appropriate.

## SEC. 1009. INAPPLICABILITY OF CERTAIN ADMINISTRATIVE PROVISIONS.

**(a) FEDERAL ADVISORY COMMITTEE ACT.—**

The provisions of the Federal Advisory Committee Act (5 U.S.C. App.) shall not apply to the activities of the Commission under this title.

**(b) FREEDOM OF INFORMATION ACT.—**

The provisions of section 552 of title 5, United States Code (commonly referred to as the Freedom of Information Act), shall not apply to the activities, records, and proceedings of the Commission under this title.

**[SEC. 1010. Repealed**. Pub. L. 111-259, title VII, § 701(b)(3), Oct. 7, 2010, 124 Stat. 2745.]

## SEC. 1011. DEFINITIONS.
In this title:
(1) CONGRESSIONAL INTELLIGENCE COMMITTEES.—
The term "congressional intelligence committees" means—
(A) the Select Committee on Intelligence of the Senate; and
(B) the Permanent Select Committee on Intelligence of the House of Representatives.
(2) INTELLIGENCE COMMUNITY.— The term "intelligence community" has the meaning given that term in section 3(4) of the National Security Act of 1947 (50 U.S.C. 401a(4)).

2. **Legislation establishing the Director of Science and Technology within the Office of the Director of National Intelligence (50 *U.S.C.* § 403-3e)**

## § 403-3e. Director of Science and Technology
**(a) Director of Science and Technology**
There is a Director of Science and Technology within the Office of the Director of National Intelligence who shall be appointed by the Director of National Intelligence.
Page 107 TITLE 50—WAR AND NATIONAL DEFENSE § 403-3g
**(b) Requirement relating to appointment**
An individual appointed as Director of Science and Technology shall have a professional background and experience appropriate for the duties of the Director of Science and Technology.
**(c) Duties**
The Director of Science and Technology shall—
(1) act as the chief representative of the Director of National Intelligence for science and technology;
(2) chair the Director of National Intelligence Science and Technology Committee under subsection (d) of this section;
(3) assist the Director in formulating a long-term strategy for scientific advances in the field of intelligence;
(4) assist the Director on the science and technology elements of the budget of the Office of the Director of National Intelligence; and
(5) perform other such duties as may be prescribed by the Director of National Intelligence or specified by law.
**(d) Director of National Intelligence Science and Technology Committee**
(1) There is within the Office of the Director of Science and Technology a Director of National Intelligence Science and Technology Committee.
(2) The Committee shall be composed of the principal science officers of the National Intelligence Program.
(3) The Committee shall—
(A) coordinate advances in research and development related to intelligence; and
(B) perform such other functions as the Director of Science and Technology shall prescribe.

3. **Legislation extending the Commission**
Pub. L. 112-277 (Jan. 24, 2013; 126 Stat. 2466)

## § 502. EXTENSION OF NATIONAL COMMISSION FOR THE REVIEW OF THE RESEARCH AND DEVELOPMENT PROGRAMS OF THE UNITED STATES INTELLIGENCE COMMUNITY.

Section 1007(a) of the Intelligence Authorization Act for Fiscal Year 2003 (Public Law 107–306; 50 U.S.C. 401 note) is amended by striking "Not later than one year after the date on which all members of the Commission are appointed pursuant to section 701(a)(3) of the Intelligence Authorization Act for Fiscal Year 2010," and inserting "Not later than March 31, 2013,".

# List of Briefings

The Commissioners and staff of the National Commission for the Review of Research and Development Programs of the United States Intelligence Community would like to express our sincere gratitude to the individuals that met with us, and the individuals that participated in the numerous groups/panels listed below. Their flexibility, willingness to share important insights, and candid responses were of utmost importance to the creation of this report. This report would not be possible without their support, insightful analysis, and willingness to provide information.

**29 February 2012**

- *Office of the Director of National Intelligence*

**5 March 2012**

- *Defense Intelligence Agency*

**6 March 2012**

- *Intelligence Advanced Research Projects Activity*

**7 March 2012**

- *National Geospatial-Intelligence Agency*

**10 April 2012**

- *In-Q-Tel*

**11 April 2012**

- *Central Intelligence Agency*

**3 May 2012**

- *Collaboration Panel*

**4 May 2012**

- *Central Intelligence Agency*

**11 May 2012**

- *First Cyber Panel*

**14 May 2012**

- *National Security Agency*

**16 May 2012**

- *Defense Advanced Research Projects Agency*

**29 May 2012**

- *National Reconnaissance Office*

**30 May 2012**

- *Department of Defense Research and Engineering Enterprise*

**31 May 2012**

- *National Nuclear Security Administration*

**6 June 2012**

- *Defense Intelligence Agency*

**12 June 2012**

- *Federal Bureau of Investigation*

**13 June 2012**

- *Office of Director of National Intelligence/Systems & Resources Analysis, Intelligence, Planning, Programming, Budgeting & Evaluation*

**14 June 2012**

- *Department of Homeland Security*

**26 June 2012**

- *Office of the Director of National Intelligence/Acquisition, Technology & Facilities*

**27 June 2012**

- *Pacific Northwest National Laboratory*
- *Lawrence Livermore National Laboratory*

**12 July 2012**

- *Sandia National Laboratory*
- *Los Alamos National Laboratory*

**17 July 2012**

- *Executive Office of the President, Office of Science & Technology Policy*
- *Government Accountability Office*
- *National Academies of Science*
- *MITRE*

**19 July 2012**

- *Merck, Inc.*

**26 July 2012**
- *AT&T*

**30 July 2012**
- *IBM*

**7 August 2012**
- *S&TI Panel*

**8 August 2012**
- *Wireless Panel*
- *Former S&T Experts Panel*
- *House Armed Services Committee*
- *Department of Energy*

**16 August 2012**
- *Academic Panel*

**22 August 2012**
- *New York City Police Commissioner's Office*
- *New York City District Attorney's Office*

**27 August 2012**
- *I2WD & JIEDDO Panel*
- *Executive Office of the President, Homeland Security Advisor*
- *House Permanent Select Committee on Intelligence*
- *Senate Select Committee on Intelligence*

**29 August 2012**
- *Independent Research and Development (IRAD) Panel*

**10 September 2012**
- *O'Reilly Publishing*
- *Former S&T Experts Panel*

**11 September 2012**
- *Cloud Computing Panel*

**12 September 2012**
- *IC Science Advisory Body Experts Panel*

**14–15 September 2012**
- *Oak Ridge National Laboratory*

**19 September 2012**
- *University of Maryland (former NSF representative)*

**2 October 2012**
- *Central Intelligence Agency*

**3 October 2012**
- *National Academies of Science*

**11 October 2012**
- *Central Intelligence Agency, Lessons Learned Office*

**25 October 2012**
- *JASON scientists*

**26 October 2012**
- *Intelligence Science Board Task Force Study*

**7 November 2012**
- *MITRE*

**13–14 November 2012**
- *Sandia National Laboratory*

**15 November 2012**
- *SRI International*
- *Kleiner Perkins Kaufman Byers*
- *Lockheed Martin Applied Technology Center*

**16 November 2012**
- *Google*

**28 November 2012**
- *Intelligence Advanced Research Projects Activity*
- *Innovative Solutions Consortium*

**4 December 2012**
- *Executive Office of the President, Office of Management & Budget*

**13 December 2012**

- *National Security Agency*
- *Office of the Director of National Intelligence*

**19 December 2012**

- *B612 Foundation*
- *National Critical Systems and Technology Joint Task Force*

**9 January 2013**

- *Defense Intelligence Agency*

**15 January 2013**

- *Second Cyber Panel*

**28 January 2013**

- *IC S&T Professionals*

**31 January 2013**

- *Executive Office of the President, National Security Staff*

**5 February 2013**

- *Identity Intelligence Panel*

**12 February 2013**

- *Disruptive Technologies Panel*

**25 February 2013**

- *National Geospatial-Intelligence Agency*

**26 February 2013**

- *Director of DARPA*

**8 March 2013**

- *Deputy Secretary of Defense*

**18 March 2013**

- *National Security Agency*

**19 March 2013**

- *Georgia Tech Research Institute*
- *National Security Agency, Cyberlaw Brief*

**11 April 2013**

- *Director of the Center for Intelligence Research and Analysis*

**16 April 2013**

- *Managing Director of Cybersecurity for JP Morgan Chase*
- *Independent Consultant for Cyber Security*

# Commissioner Biographies

**Maurice Sonnenberg, Commission Co-Chair,** is the Senior International Advisor at J. P. Morgan. He has advised five presidential administrations in the fields of foreign policy, international trade, finance, and intelligence. He is currently a member of the Special Navy Advisory Panel to the Secretary of the Navy.

Some past governmental positions he has held in the fields of intelligence are member of the President's Foreign Intelligence Advisory Board (eight years), Vice Chairman of the National Commission on Terrorism, member of the U.S. Commission on Reducing and Protecting Government Secrecy, the Senior Advisor to the U.S. Commission on the Roles and Capabilities of the U.S. Intelligence Community, and member of the Private Sector Senior Advisory Committee and the Southwest Border Task Force of the Homeland Security Advisory Council. He is a member of the Council on Foreign Relations, where he served on the Council's Independent Task Force on Terrorist Financing, and is on the Advisory Board of the Council's magazine, *Foreign Affairs*.

**Samantha Ravich, Ph.D., Commission Co-Chair,** consults with both private industry and federal and state governments on international security, financial risk, and political risk. She is a Senior Advisor to the Chertoff Group. From 2009 to 2011, Ravich was Senior Vice President at IPS, a software and global analysis firm.

Ravich was previously Principal Deputy National Security Advisor to Vice President Cheney and served in the White House for 5½ years. She received a Ph.D. in policy analysis from the RAND Graduate School, an M.C.P. from the University of Pennsylvania, and a B.S.E. in finance from the Wharton School. In 2000, Cambridge University Press published Ravich's book, *Marketization and Democracy: East Asian Experiences*, which is used as a basic textbook in international economics, political science, and Asian studies courses in colleges throughout the country.

**Senator Dan Coats** is the senior senator for Indiana. Coats began his service to our nation in the U.S. Army, and has served Hoosiers in both the U.S. House of Representatives and U.S. Senate. In 2001, he was named Ambassador to Germany, arriving in the country only a few days before the tragic events of 9/11. Coats returned to the U.S. Senate in 2011. He serves on four Senate committees: Appropriations, Intelligence, Commerce, and the Joint Economic Committee, where he is the senior Senate Republican. Dan and Marsha Coats met in college and have three adult children and eight grandchildren.

**Congressman K. Michael Conaway** is a member of both the House Armed Services Committee and the House Permanent Select Committee on Intelligence. Congressman Conaway served as both the Chairman of the Panel on Defense Financial Management and Auditability Reform in the 112th Congress and the Ranking Member of the Committee's Panel on Defense Acquisition Reform in the 111th Congress. In addition, he has served on various subcommittees within the Armed Services Committee and currently sits on both the Subcommittee on Emerging Threats and Capabilities and the Subcommittee on Oversight and Investigations. On the House Permanent Select Committee on Intelligence, Congressman Conaway currently serves on the Subcommittee on Terrorism, HUMINT, Analysis, and Counterintelligence. In 2012,

Congressman Conaway was appointed to the Board of Visitors of the U.S. Military Academy at West Point.

**Representative Rush Holt** has represented central New Jersey in the U.S. House of Representatives since 1999. From 2007 to 2010, he was Chair of the Select Intelligence Oversight Panel, which worked to strengthen oversight of the Intelligence Community. He was also a senior member of the House Permanent Select Committee on Intelligence from 2003 to 2011 and previously served as an intelligence analyst at the Department of State in the 1980s. Holt holds a B.A. in physics from Carleton College and M.A. and Ph.D. degrees, also in physics, from New York University. He served on the faculty of Swarthmore College and from 1989 until his 1998 congressional campaign served as Assistant Director of the Princeton Plasma Physics Laboratory, the largest research facility of Princeton University and the largest center for alternative energy research in New Jersey. He is a resident of Hopewell Township, New Jersey.

**The Honorable Shirley Ann Jackson, Ph.D.,** is President of Rensselaer Polytechnic Institute (RPI), and has held senior leadership positions in government, industry, research, and academe. From 1995 to 1999, Dr. Jackson served as Chairman of the U.S. Nuclear Regulatory Commission. She serves on the President's Council of Advisors on Science and Technology (PCAST) and the International Security Advisory Board (ISAB) to the United States Department of State. Dr. Jackson is an International Fellow of the Royal Academy of Engineering and a member of the National Academy of Engineering and a number of other professional societies. She is a Regent of the Smithsonian Institution, a member of the boards of the Council on Foreign Relations and the Brookings Institution, and a member of the Board of Directors of IBM, FedEx, and other global companies. Dr. Jackson holds an S.B. degree in physics and a Ph.D. in theoretical physics, both from MIT.

**Gilman Louie** is a partner of Alsop Louie Partners, a venture capital fund focused on helping entrepreneurs start companies, and the founder and first CEO of In-Q-Tel, a private nonprofit venture capital firm that invests in private companies on behalf of a wide range of U.S. intelligence agencies. Before founding In-Q-Tel, he ran a publicly traded company called Spectrum HoloByte; it ultimately was acquired by Hasbro Corporation, where he served as chief creative officer of Hasbro Interactive and general manager of Games.com. He serves a member of the Board of Directors of the Markle Foundation and of Digital Promise, and is Chairman of the Board of the Federation of American Scientists. Gilman is also an advisor to the Defense Intelligence Agency, Central Intelligence Agency, and National Security Agency, and is a member of the Technical Advisory Group to the United States Senate Select Committee on Intelligence.

**Kevin P. Meiners** is the Deputy Under Secretary of Defense for Intelligence for Strategy, Programs, and Resources, where he is responsible for all matters related to Intelligence, Surveillance & Reconnaissance, and Environmental system capabilities. Mr. Meiners began his government service in 1984, working in various engineering, aviation, and program management–related positions before joining the Office of the Secretary of Defense in 1994 as a member of the newly formed Defense Airborne Reconnaissance Office (DARO); in 2000 he became a member of the Senior Executive Service. He has a BSEE from Virginia Tech

University and holds two Master of Science degrees; he is also a graduate of the Federal Executive Institute.

**The Honorable Stephanie O'Sullivan,** as the Principal Deputy Director of National Intelligence (PDDNI) since 28 February 2011, serves the Intelligence Community in a role similar to that of a chief operating officer, focusing on ODNI operations; managing IC coordination, information sharing, and resource challenges; and reinforcing the DNI's intelligence integration initiatives. Beginning in 2005, Ms. O'Sullivan led the CIA's Directorate of Science and Technology (DS&T), the part of the Agency responsible for developing and deploying innovative technology in support of intelligence collection and analysis, and she served as Associate Deputy Director of the CIA from December 2009 through February 2011. Previously, as an engineer and team leader with the CIA, the Office of Naval Intelligence, and TRW, she fielded systems in areas ranging from power sources to biotechnology. She holds a Bachelor of Science degree in civil engineering from the Missouri University of Science and Technology.

**Troy E. Wade II** is chairman emeritus of the Nevada Alliance for Defense, Energy and Business, a group of more than 35 technology companies that support the Nevada Test Site and help bring new science and technlgy programs to Nevada, and president and chairman of the Nevada Test Site Historical Foundation. He is also president of Wade Associates, a Las Vegas–based management consulting firm. Mr. Wade is a member of the Board of Directors of WSI, Inc.; a member of the Advisory Board of TSC, Inc.; a member of the Advisory Board of Longenecker & Associates; and a member of the Advisory Board of the Howard R. Hughes School of Engineering at the University of Nevada, Las Vegas.

Mr. Wade has 31 years of service with the U.S. Department of Energy, having served as Assistant Secretary of Energy for Defense Programs after holding a succession of key positions associated with the nation's nuclear programs.

**Senator Mark Warner** was elected to the U.S. Senate in November 2008; he serves on the Senate Banking, Budget, Commerce, and Intelligence committees. After more than four years in the Senate, Senator Warner has established himself as a national leader in efforts to find bipartisan consensus to create balanced solutions to reduce the federal debt and deficit. He also has been a champion for military men and women, their families, and our military veterans. Senator Warner also is a leader in Congress in efforts to promote private-sector innovation and to help our nation's small businesses and start-up companies succeed.

From 2002 to 2006, Senator Warner served as Governor of Virginia, where he worked in a bipartisan way to turn record budget deficits into a surplus. Governor Warner also focused on improving public education and expanding economic opportunity in every region of the state. Before entering public office, Senator Warner was an early investor in the cellular telephone business. He co-founded the company that became Nextel, and ultimately made early investments in hundreds of start-up technology companies that have created tens of thousands of private-sector jobs.

**The Honorable John J. Young, Jr.,** served as the Under Secretary of Defense for Acquisition, Technology and Logistics, with responsibility for all research, development, procurement, and logistics programs in the Department of Defense. During his tenure, he drove DOD initiatives on competitive prototyping, revision of the DOD 5000 instruction, and collaborative program management. Previously, Mr. Young oversaw DOD's research enterprise as the Director of Defense Research and Engineering and led the Mine Resistant Ambush Protected (MRAP) Vehicle Task Force, which delivered more than 15,000 MRAPs to protect soldiers from improvised explosive devices (IEDs).

Mr. Young also served as the Assistant Secretary of the Navy for Research, Development and Acquisition and worked for ten years as a professional staff member of the Senate Defense Appropriations Subcommittee. He currently serves as a board member, advisor, and consultant to a number of companies.

# Acknowledgments

This Commission depended on and would like to thank the extraordinary staff that dedicated themselves to the yearlong venture. Staff members demonstrated exemplary interagency collaboration in performing their assessments on behalf of the Commission, supporting the Commissioners' vision for improving research across the entire national intelligence enterprise, and bringing to fruition the final report.

The Commission is profoundly grateful to all of the staff and to all individuals who enabled the completion of its report.